1st Edition - 101 Questions for Business Owners

ISBN: 978-0-244-72948-6

I0474464

"Strength doesn't come from what you can do.
Strength comes from overcoming things you thought
you couldn't."

Unknown

"In the business world you are paid in two coins:
cash and experience.
Take the experience first; the cash will come later"

Harold S Geenen

Introduction Bit

I am a business coach. There…I said it.

Well. This is good. You haven't dropped the book and run off screaming yet. So, let's talk some more.

I believe a significant part of coaching is asking questions so that I can understand where your weaknesses lie so we can then move through them. Where your strengths can be further improved. Resulting in progress for you and your business.

But it's also a coach's job to ask those questions and then get you to hear the answers to them, and then maybe get you to delve a little deeper into those answers in the context of whatever we're talking about. It's key you 'hear' the answers to those questions. By hearing I mean, actually taking notice, responsibility and ownership of the answers.

As humans we love certainty. We love to be certain that everything is right, in its place and where it should be. Strangely we also like uncertainty. We like surprises. Actually, we lie to ourselves with regard to that. We like surprises when it's a 'nice surprise' and not when our partner walks out with the kids and the dog.

In general, we are all happy to listen to positive answers to questions. Such as, "Are you brilliant at what you do?", "Yes, you are"

But none of us is very good at hearing this answer to the same question; "You are good, but you could do this, this and this to be brilliant."

Many of us will hang on to the "You are good..." and then mutter under our breath about the fact they didn't think we were brilliant. Not many people would listen to the "...But you could do this, this and this..." bit of the conversation.

And that's a shame. Because successful businesses listen to those nuggets of information, act upon them and grow themselves and their businesses because of them.

So, when I wrote this there were 75 questions I originally asked of my business and of myself. As you can see these increased by another 26 when I found that I wanted to drill down even more and be as honest with myself as I could be.

What I then found is that these same questions became hugely beneficial and staple in the businesses I was coaching. They encourage an honesty within people.

There are some questions that perhaps sound similar, but they aren't. They are designed to make you read them once, twice, maybe three times. Some are written to make you look at an original question in a very different way. Richard Branson, Lord Sugar and even God will appear at some point.

Answer honestly and openly.

The beauty of these business reflections is that when you recognise potential weaknesses you start to move forward on them. Jump forward three months and you look at this book again and at your original answers, you'll probably find the answers have now changed or your perspective of the answer has changed.

Answer the questions in one go or one per day. Do what's right for you but answer honestly. You are not trying to impress anyone. You're not in a competition with anyone else. Just you.

Enjoy completing the book. Enjoy the 'time out' you will get by working through this book. Taking a few minutes, a day to think about an answer is usually a large step forward into improving you and the business. Here's the thing...you've already started...you've got to the end of this.

Enjoy the ride,

Marc
Your Best Kept Business Secret

1 What business are you in?

This is a very relevant question. Why?

Well, the answer may seem obvious to some, but not to others. The whole purpose of a business is to be a problem solver. I want someone to calculate how much I owe in tax...an accountant can do that. I want some beans in a tomato sauce...a manufacturer of tins of beans can do that. I want someone to help guide me in my business...I can help you with that; (sorry couldn't resist!).

Potential clients and customers have problems and they need a service or a product to solve that problem. Some customers and clients don't actually know they have a problem and that's when the difficulty rears its head through marketing and sales. Essentially though every business, service provider or product delivers a solution to a problem.

Reflecting on what business you are ACTUALLY in; will help you gain a clearer focus on how you can help those customers and clients out there.

2 Where do you make your money?

I once worked with a guy who called himself a coach. He actually did very little coaching. What he did do was sell lots of online courses.

Although he did do some 'coaching' within these courses, I challenged him about his title. I asked him, "Do you consider yourself an online course builder?"

He'd missed it. A fresh eye at what he did meant that I could see he was a 'business course' developer and they were good courses too. I wanted him to change his outlook on where he made his money and it worked.

He repositioned his marketing and increased his business by over 200% in less than two months. This shows that taking a step back to refocus on what you actually make money from; will help you move your business forward by doing more of it and making it even better.

Not everyone should diversify if that means they cannot focus on the core parts of the business that makes them money.

3 Is my product / service a real business?

Is this an odd question? I don't think so.

I think it's legitimate. The amount of guru's and people who say "Find something you like to do, and you'll never work another day..."

To a point that's true but knitting jumpers for Polar Bears probably isn't the greatest business decision ever, because there is simply no need.

You have to ask yourself this question not in terms of whether you'll become a multi-millionaire overnight, but rather in terms of whether it can provide you with enough income to pay the bills and put food on the table.

I've seen many people in multi-level-marketing schemes be 'sold a dream', but very few ever get to live it. Your business will take blood, sweat and tears. Long days and short nights. Tantrums and sleepless nights. Consider the effort that will need to be put into your product or service to make it 'pay the bills', before you think of those holidays you've always dreamed of.

4 How good are you at your competitive positions?

If you are a premium brand, does everything you communicate physically, marketing or online reflect that premium brand?

If you are a budget brand, are you just that?

Or are bits of your business venturing all over the place and leaving mixed messages?

Are your price points, value points and service points reflecting your position in the market?

Get a fresh pair of eyes to look at your marketing, website and social media. You could be sending out the right messages, but poorly or the wrong messages, really well.

Go from the point of view of what you want the message to be and then reflect on how clear it would be for a new client or customer.

5 Is this a good industry to be in?

What will your mates and family say? What do the papers and financial journals say?

If you go back a decade, people hated bankers. Not the guys behind the glass counters in the branch, but the ones behind the glass windows in the cities. Was it a good industry to be in? Depends how you looked at it.

If you were ethical and did things properly, then there were frustrations because a minority made your life difficult. I've read and heard many stories about people leaving that industry at that time to set up new, very different businesses; many of which have become successful. Not only financially, but probably emotionally rewarding as well.

Do you want to become a driving instructor for example? What is your strategy for when automated cars go into mass circulation?

Do you want to own a coffee shop? How are you going to deal with the masses that are already on the high street?

Think back to question 3. Will your industry be able to support you in good times and bad?

6 What do your clients think?

A difficult question to answer unless you ask them.

Businesses are frightened of honest feedback. Treat it as a free gift of knowledge. Without it, you won't know what you're doing right and what you're doing wrong.

Now if you're doing something wrong, or something is being miscommunicated, you now have the chance to put it right and delight your customers and clients.

Questionnaires, surveys, telephone calls, asking for reviews, etc., should all be part of your business strategy every day, every week, every month you are in business.

7 How do you raise profits quickly?

You've sat and looked at last year's accounts. You are going number blind by looking at the incomings and outgoings on your bank statements. How can you improve the profit you get from the sales of your products or services?

Is it as simple as putting your prices up? (Sometimes that is an effective marketing tool.)

Or, when was the last time you reviewed all your costs and expenses? A bit like car insurance and utilities. A large proportion of the population let these run and run, even though by shopping around they could save themselves hundreds if not thousands of pounds by moving to another provider, without losing the quality of cover or service.

Small businesses struggle with this too. Now I'm not asking you to run around 'screwing everyone' on their prices, but I'm asking you to negotiate fairly if you've been in a business relationship for a while.

Write down ideas and thoughts on how you can raise your profits quickly...

8 How do you build long-term value?

Relationships with customers and clients should never be one hit wonders. And yes, that includes undertakers.

One of the cheapest tools of marketing is building long-term value for ALL your customers and clients. This should mean different levels of services and products before and after purchases.

They could be a simple blog or e-letter, right up to after sales care and consultation after a purchase. What will make your customers and clients return to you every time they have a need for your products or services?

9 Who / What business inspires your business?

A long time ago, I met a business coach who 'coached' his clients to the point that they began to lie to him about what they had achieved. They even damaged their client's mental health as they relentlessly made them chase targets and goals in the pursuit of financial goals. I heard stories about others rigidly staying to someone else's '12 Step Programme', come hell or high water so that they could 'achieve a headline number' to impress potential clients.

I became a coach because I recognised something very early on. Other businesses are as unique as the fingerprints on their hands. Yes, there are basics that every business should follow, but outside of that, it's about being different, unique and a journey of growth. Growth for the business owner and then the business; because without the owner, there is no business.

That's what inspires me when I coach, when I write and when I present. I've helped those businesses to 'right the top-heavy building' that they call their business, by taking the time to put the right foundations in place, so now they can continue to grow at a rate that pleases them and not their coach.

So why do you do what you do? There is never a bad time to reconnect with your inspirations. So, do it now…

10 What do you do differently from other businesses?

I've spoken with hundreds of business owners in the last couple of years and they love to tell me what they do and how they do it. Tellingly, only a few tell me why they do it...what or who has inspired them to own their own business.

More worryingly though is the lack of knowledge of what their competition actually does. One of the very first tasks I ask people to partake in is a SWOT analysis of the competition, both nationally and locally. Why?

A lot of owners 'think' they know what's going on, by hearsay and glancing at websites but very, very few dig any deeper than that. I'll give you an example of why you should spend some time finding out what exactly you do differently.

In every driving test centre up and down the land, there is a driving instructor that sits in the corner waiting for the pupil to get back from their practical test. They seem to have been around for 'donkey's years'. They are the wise ones. They have seen other instructors come and go and all the changes that go with the industry. They are incredibly vocal in what will and won't work in the industry; some of it with merit, but they are also the first to tell you how busy they are and how they are charging the top rate in the area because they have the most first time passes.

Imagine your surprise as when you go out and about on your daily business, you become very aware that you seem to see their car, 'L plates' and headboard adorned, always on the driveway outside their home. Then imagine your complete surprise when, whilst posing as a parent of a new pupil, they inform you that not only do they not offer several vital services you do, they are in fact the cheapest instructor in the area and have loads of room in their diary to get your fictitious child started.

Moral of the story? Go find out what you really do differently to others. What you consider a 'run of the mill' part of your service could act as a genuine 'unique selling point' when it comes to comparisons between you and others. You may even find out you've been charging too little for your products and services, because of the extra value that you offer compared to others.

As for the things you recognise that you might not do so well at, it's a golden opportunity to put those things right quickly. But if you don't spend the time to find out, how are you ever really going to know?

11 What investments underpin your differences?

So, this is why the last question was quite important. If you know your differences and how they can help drive you and your business forward, what are you doing to make them even better than your competition?

On the flip side, what investment of time, skill or knowledge are you making to help support those differences by tending to the weaknesses so that they can become critical foundations to your business?

If you are about to answer this question with the word 'nothing', then perhaps use the rest of the page to start jotting down a plan of action.

12 What are your key sources of competitive advantage?

So, where have these key advantages come from?

If you're a small business is your key competitive advantage your size? And trust me, size doesn't matter unless you let it. Imagine being a big business and having to go through endless meetings, conversations with directors, emails and phone calls just to change one key aspect of a business. What a ball ache! If you're a small business you can change direction almost as quickly as the wind, because the only person that needs to be satisfied are your customers, clients and you.

Imagine if a client or customer wants something in a particular style or flavour. Can you 'source it' quickly if you wanted to? Again, in big business, they'd have to go through chains of command and endless emails and calls to get it done. A small business could get it done in less than 24 hours if they put their backs into it.

On the flip side, if you are a big business, you have buying power and a network of people to get things done efficiently, again if people put their minds to it. They could also have the backing of a better, well-known brand name.

So where have you got key competitive advantages and how can you make them better, faster and stronger so you can continue to delight your clients and customers?

13 What do you need to do to make a difference?

You can take this question in various ways, and it's entirely up to you. Remember that I've said that every business and their owners are unique? Well, this is one of those questions because it's a reflection of your goals and visions for you and your business.

If you want to make a difference personally, what do you need to do?
If you want your business to change the way people do business, what do you need to do?
If you want to leave a legacy, what do you need to do?
If you want to earn a million pounds a donate it to charity what do you need to do?

Answer this question in as many ways as you want. The answers are all about you and what you NEED to do to make a difference no matter how small.

14 What must you keep?

These will be very personal answers.

What are the best aspects of you, your habits, your strategies and processes must you keep to get you to your vision and goals for you and your business?

Is it drive, determination and focus? Or creativity, inspiration and motivation?

15 What must you lose?

We all know things we need to stop doing or get rid of. So, what are those things?

Do you have a 'mood hoover' in your life that always brings you and your ideas down? The kind of person that if they won the lottery, they'd moan it still wasn't quite enough. They suck the life out of a room when they walk into it. Then lose them now.

I want you to think and write down things that are holding you back and yes, that includes friends too. You are the sum of the closest five people to you, so if they are all doom and gloom merchants...get rid!

If you're wasting time binge-watching box-sets on streaming platforms instead of working and growing your business, then get rid of the platform or restrict your viewing.

If you're expecting miracle cures, a guaranteed shortcut to success or want overnight fame, then you need to get rid of that too. Because silver bullets only exist in horror movies with werewolves.

16 How could you simplify your business so that you can raise its value by 50%?

What extras are there in the business that is just there for the sake of it?

What are you actually paying for when it comes to being able to deliver your service?

Where is the excess fat that may be costing you thousands of pounds a year?

How simple and productive are your working arrangements now?

17 How could you simplify your business so that you could lower your costs by 10%?

This might take some thought, but when was the last time you reviewed your costs, or do you leave that to other people to decide?

Get involved with the numbers and work out whether you can reduce costs by 10%, WITHOUT damaging the quality of services and products you supply.

18 Is your strategy rather complex? Aren't all successful businesses strategies very simple?

Reflect on whether you are getting to your existing or prospective customers and clients easily.

It's true, there is so much 'business and marketing noise' out there that some people come up with long-winded strategies, just so that they can be heard above everybody else's noise. Funnels, tunnels and boxes are phrases banded around by marketing types who make some things far more complicated than they need to be. But is that the right thing to do?

Are there other ways you could be connecting with partners, customers, clients and influencers that are far simpler and more cost-effective? Sometimes just knocking on someone's door and asking if they have time for a coffee is far easier than sending 8 emails and leaving 20 voicemails.

19 What is the key idea to your business concept?

What is the ONE thing that makes you and your business attractive?

Apple led with "Your entire record collection in your pocket." Now there was a concept...

20 Who is your target client?

Now I'm not going to apologise for the next set of 7 questions. EVERY, and I mean EVERY business should have a handle on this stuff.

Why? Because if you're marketing to everyone, you are marketing to no-one. If you're selling anything to everyone, you are selling the wrong stuff to no-one.

Write down a brief description of them now, without thinking about it or moving forward.

21 What do you know about them?

Have you ever studied what your ideal customer is?

What do they want?

What do they need?

What do they earn?

Think of your last three clients or customers. What were they like? Describe them.

22 Can you describe your perfect client in detail?

Start with a blank sheet of paper.

Are they male or female?
What age are they?
What do they earn?
What do they do?
Married/divorced?

Describe them in as much detail as you want to help you clarify your focus. If you're in business to business, describe the owner in as much detail as you can and then describe the size, shape, niche, etc., of the business.

Having a clear mental image of who they are will only aid you in attracting them constantly.

23 Where do they hang out?

Now please don't go stalking them, but is your ideal client and customer on LinkedIn or Facebook? Pinterest or Instagram? YouTube or Vevo?

Golf club or social club? Bar or Pub? Private networking groups or free local ones? National or local events? Niche fayres or national conventions?

Again, it's where you need to refocus your efforts to get in front of these ideal clients and customers.

24 What do they read?

Do they read the Economist, The Daily Mail or the Daily Star?

Do they read books, magazines or comics?

If you put an old-fashioned advert in something they read, where would be the ideal place to put it that would attract their attention?

If you wrote a book or reviewed a book, would they read it?

If you write blogs, where do they find you from?

25 How do they interact socially?

Everyone HAS to be on social media. Why? Because social media 'experts' say so.

Whilst its partly true, people do tend to hang out with other people in reality also. So where do they go to relax and unwind or where do they go to meet other like-minded people like themselves?

Do they 'do business' on the Golf Course or at networking events? Do they go to clubs or groups?

What social media do they actively use? Is it LinkedIn or Facebook? Twitter or Instagram? If you don't know, go and find out!

26 What problems are you solving for your customers?

Every business is a problem solver. Fact.

So what problems can your business solve for your ideal customers and clients?

How much will it make their life better and why will it make it better than before?

(Pro Tip: If you write down 10 problems, when you next go to a networking event and someone is there doing the same as you, by having 10 problems in the locker that you can deal with, you can use one of them to make your 1 minute or 40 second pitch different and unique!)

27 How much power do your clients and customers have over your business?

If a client doesn't turn up for a meeting and pay for something, what will that do to your mood for the day?

If 20% of your clients left today, how long would your business run for before having to replace them?

Are you running around after them trying to please them or are you aiming to please them as they approach you?

28 Why do people buy your products or services at all?

Why? Just why?

Don't make stuff up here. Find out if you don't know.

Ask current or past clients and customers... NOW!

29 Why do people buy your product or services from you?

Now unless you are a Bill Gates or a Steve Jobs type of person here, I'm going to assume that you are not the only person to do what you do and sell what you sell.

So, what is it about YOU that makes people part with their money and give it to your business?

30 Which clients are cool?

Write down the clients and customers you have the most fun with. The ones that are a pleasure to see and a pleasure to work with.

Name them if you wish so you can get a clearer mental image of them.

31 Which clients drive you mad?

Name them if you wish.

Again, this will give you a clear mental image of who to avoid.

32 Should you be working with them?

Honest answers, please. And if it's because of cashflow, etc., that you are working with them what might they be holding you back from?

33 What benefits are you offering that your competition doesn't?

You should only answer this if you've done a full and detailed competitor SWOT analysis.

Otherwise, it's just a guess and a story you tell other people to make you feel better about your business.

34 If you could use just two sentences to describe what your business stands for, what would they be?

Notice it says, 'stands for' and NOT 'what it does.

Other people do what you do. Very few will do what you do for the same reasons. It's something unique to you.

35 What is your company known for?

You may think you know, but do you really? What is the honest feedback from past clients and customers?

If you're trying to say 'one thing' to your customers, but they are hearing and seeing 'something different', then you need to take some action to correct it.

36 What's your value proposition to clients that they can't get elsewhere?

This should come from a detailed SWOT analysis of your competitors or something that you know with absolute 100% certainty that clients can't get from elsewhere or is in short supply.

What is unique to your business that the customers and clients can't get anywhere else?

37 Who are your most profitable clients?

Who would you love to be able to replicate, roll them up and take them everywhere with you?

Think about how you got them. Think about how they were attracted to you and your business.

What products and services do they buy and why?

What can you learn from them?

38 At what rate do they leave you?

When a customer goes it hurts. So, at what rate are you noticing people leave and perhaps go elsewhere

39 Why do they leave you?

This can be irrelevant for some businesses. When someone dies, the Undertaker may not be expecting repeat business from the deceased.

When a learner driver passes their driving test, the instructor would be very unlikely to see them in their driver's seat again unless they've been a very naughty boy or girl and lose their license.

So, when was the last time you found out why a customer or client went elsewhere or just stopped using your services?

Do you have a system in place to track these events?

Could it have been prevented?

What can you do to reward existing customers and clients to be able to keep them?

40 Who is your most serious competitor?

Many different answers to this one probably.

From a big national competitor to big local businesses.

Also, consider the 'people' involved. Is the 'owner' of a business your competitor or is it really 'you' that you're in competition with?

41 What are their plans?

80% of your competition do little or no updating of their skills and industry knowledge unless they have to.

If you read one industry book or magazine, you're already ahead of the majority. So how else can you keep up with what's happening in your industry or niche unless you actually research it?

Businesses hate doing SWOT analysis, but if you want to move forward, revisiting a SWOT and making it a living breathing thing is essential for any form of success.

42 Do you really know what clients think of you?

Where is the evidence to back this up?

Are you accepting of negative reviews as much as positive ones?

What do your customer surveys say about you, and how do you use the information to make progress?

43 Is the customer, always right?

Trickier than it looks this.

Perhaps personal opinions and prejudices get in the way here. But if something has gone wrong and the customer feels the need to complain, is it simply because of processes or is it about communication and expectations of both the business and the customer.

Become a customer service analyser and look at how 'mistakes' in the process can be rectified for future. At the same time whilst you want to amaze and please people, you should fully understand your own rights when it comes to transactions between you and customers.

44 What are your competitor's costs and profits?

Difficult information to find, granted. This will require some serious detective work but imagine your amazement if you find out they are getting a better deal from the same supplier as you.

You then have a platform to negotiate.

You may find their suppliers are better than yours, offering more value and service.

If you don't go and look, you'll never know.

45 Who are currently your new / minor threats?

You should look a little deeper at this question by understanding that although these businesses or set of circumstances are currently new and minor, it won't take long to become established and big threats.

It relates back to my long-held belief that a SWOT analysis should be a living and breathing document as things can change quickly. New players with different perspectives on business in your niche and industry, will come and go. Stand still on the right road long enough, you'll eventually get run over.

46 Are you supplying the right things?

Is there a product or service that just isn't moving, shifting or selling?

Then ask yourself this question: Why do you offer it?

Does it make you any money?

Is it cluttering up your website, your a store or office?

Does anyone actually know about it?

Can it be 'repackaged' and put with other products or services?

What could you be offering that offers value to potential customers and clients that you aren't offering right now?

What does your competitor offer that you could offer better than them?

What does your competitor offer that you don't, and you must offer if you are to survive?

47 And the most effective way?

At the time of writing this 40% of small businesses, DON'T have a website! I know…right?!

But here's the thing, with technology the way it is, are you offering the sale of your products and services in the most easiest and convenient way?

If it's a service, what is expected by the customer or client and what are the 'follow-up's' in place to make sure they're happy?

48 At the lowest possible economic cost?

With the increase in how we use technology in everyday lives, are you providing your products or services at the lowest economic costs?

Are there costs that can be dismissed, reduced or replaced, WITHOUT losing the quality that it possesses?

Coaching as an example is moving through to apps, websites and online programmes. That will never replace 1:1 coaching but offers an alternative. We can even go further by doing the 1:1 coaching via internet call systems, which means we can even do it in our pyjamas.

So, have you removed all the obstacles in your production, sales and service process so you are making the maximum profit on your product or service?

49 How much does your business use technology in comparison with your competitors?

Have your competitors got apps?

Can your competitor's customers and clients purchase things online?

Do you have tutorials, downloads, guides and value-added information available for your customers to consume online?

Do competitors use better stock and order systems?

Are you using technology as a sales tool or a productivity tool? How can it be bettered?

50 Are your assumptions in the last set of questions, still valid? When did you last check?

If nothing else the questions may have made you go and check before you got here. Good.

If they haven't, the fact that you are making assumptions isn't a great thing. Yes, in business you will have to make some assumptions, but when it is possible, with a little time and effort to make certain you are doing things to the best of your ability and within your budget, it is absolutely necessary you do it.

51 If your business were to win an award, what would it win it for?

In recent times there has been a surge in 'award winning businesses', '#1 Amazon Best-sellers' and 'industry leading' accolades.

Some are genuine. Nominated and voted for by the public. Others won with nominations written by paid-for companies and then won because you know the person running them well enough and bought a table for ten at the over-priced three course meal shindig, during the evening. (And breathe)

But let's assume for a moment that you are being nominated by your customers for an award.

And you are judged on those merits by a panel of peers in your industry.

What would your business win an award for?
What's world class and better than the rest about it?
What would you like to be remembered for?

52 How much power do your suppliers have over your business?

If a supplier of goods or services to you, jacked their prices up by 10% what kind of affect would that have over your business?

If the answer is very little…well done you.

But if this scenario would damage your business and profits, then you my friend, have a problem.

At the very least you would have to put up prices or accept significantly reduced income and profit.

What can you do in the event of suppliers increasing their prices to you and have you got a backup plan to prevent the knock-on effects?

53 Are you as good, or better than your best competitor?

This may be a very personal question.
This may be down to the size of your bank balance, your staff or building.

It should incorporate many aspects of your business. From sales to profit. From physical size to online reach. From product range to availability. From customer service to customer retention.

This is where market research and competitor analysis are vastly important. And if you're still not getting the message...how can you answer this question unless you KNOW?

Otherwise, you are missing out on attracting new customers and clients because you might be missing valuable information for your marketing toolkit.

54 Are you serving the widest possible market?

What is your online presence like?

What is your delivery/home delivery process like? Do you have one?

Who else could you be offering your products and services to that would gain you extra, profitable income?

55 Are you in some way unique? Is there a reason why people should buy from you rather than someone else?

What is your USP?

If you've been doing some research, you may find your USP isn't AS unique as you thought...

So...

56 Would your God have a laugh at your marketing plan?

Not designed to offend, but if there was a higher power, would he or she laugh at your marketing plan for the next month, 3 months, 6 months and year?

You have got one, right?

Why would they laugh?

Why wouldn't they laugh?

57 What keeps you awake at night about your business?

Write down all your business worries here.

Part of the process of getting through them and overcoming them is writing them down and owning them. Here is as good a place as any.

58 What are your objectives for your business?

I want you to write down the results you want from your business in the next three months.

Day-to-day business sometimes gets in the way of achieving those objectives. We end up in a cycle of day-to-day and in 'survival mode'.

So, take a minute. Look at what objectives you want to achieve in the next three months, and next to each one write a short, sharp description of how you're going to do it.

59 What are you trying to achieve in the next 12 months?

"This time next year Rodney, we'll be millionaires"
Del Boy, Only Fools and Horses, BBC TV.

Where are you going to be in a years' time? Are you going to be in exactly the same place you are right now or are there things, goals and objectives you really want to achieve and move you forward?

It staggers me how many people firstly, don't look back at the last twelve months and see what they did well. Then look at what didn't work and why it didn't work. We are creatures of habit and for some reason, we like to keep making the same mistakes we have over and over again.

Secondly, some business owners develop the 'siege mentality' and in their own heads are just happy to get through the next twelve months. Which starts a cycle. Because at the end of those twelve months they've tricked themselves into believing that's the way forward. They end up pedaling hard and going absolutely nowhere.

So, take a minute. Write down your turnover in 12 months. The profit. The number of customers, employees, reviews, recommendations, products and services you have. What does this business now look like? Where does it sit in your industry or in your community?

How hard have you worked to get it there? Are they stretching targets or are they targets that are ridiculous?

What do you feel like in 12 months' time? How are you working? How are you living? Do you work more or less than today?

Be as creative and as imaginative as you want within reason. Just write it down. As soon as you do, you begin to take ownership of those aims.

60 What are you trying to achieve in the next 3 years?

This one is quite important. Things change.

In fact, we are living in a world that is changing so fast, it's becoming tricky to keep up. Just look at what your phone can do now as opposed to 3 or five years ago. Kids go from being sweet aged 10 to utter monster teenagers at 13.

Here's something to consider. Your children, (or ones that you know), will more likely do jobs that are yet to be invented. Scary isn't it?

So, the nearest to a long-term plan in present-day conditions is a 3 year one. So much will change past that and so much can change in your industry or niche during those three years. Economics, technology, laws, governments, rules have all been in a state of flux for the last 10 years, and that won't end soon. So, these achievements and goals you write down here are as near to a solid plan as you're going to get. Be brave, be smart, be bold.

61 What is the vision for your business in 5 years?

You are now thinking, what on God's great earth is he now talking about? He's just said there was no point in doing a plan for five years.

I'd say that's true with your business, but I'd like you to think about something a little closer to home. You and your family.

Earlier I said that kids can grow up so fast. My lad has gone from starting Secondary School to his final year with exams in the blink of an eye. You end up saying "Where did time go?".

So, within the blink of an eye, things change. And so, will life. What does your life look like in five years? Have you sold the business? Have you got work/life balance? Do you have weekends off? Nice holidays every year. Mortgage free, debt free? Have you got money put away for pensions or the kid's University fees?

How many branches have you got? How much is it turning over to give you this life that you want in 5 years' time? Who's running it day-to-day? What impact has it had on your customers? How much of an impact has it had on the local communities?

Write down what it looks like.

62 What barriers are in your way to achieve your goals in the next 12 months?

What is in your sights that may stop you from achieving your 12-month goal?

What threats are you aware of to your business or industry that could damage your business?

63 What will enable you to overcome the barriers, and/or achieve your goals?

What can you do right now or in the immediate future to negate any issues that may arise?

Think of things that even if barriers do come up, you can limit the impact of the damage they do to your goals.

64 If you had a magic wand, what changes would you make to your business?

Now, this is a very personal answer, but some would say that if you focus on them, the Universe will deliver. On the other hand, some would say that's b@@@@@@s!

None-the-less a question that you can have some fun with or take a bit more seriously.

65 What is stopping you from making those magic wand changes now?

You didn't think I was going to let that go, did you?

Having a 'Clear Mental Image' of where you're going, and how you're going to go about it is very, very important to business success. So, some of this 'magic wand stuff' is actually very, very achievable if you focus on it.

Many have been surprised before and many will be surprised in the future by the power of focus and clear mental images. So please...answer the question!

66 Are all incentives aligned with your business goals?

How can people help you achieve your business goals?

This is an interesting one and requires a bit of a story.

We all know about the 'PPI Scandal' that banks have been at the heart of? One of the biggest contributory factors to the problems that were caused was down to remuneration of the salesperson.

What do I mean by this? Actually, the idea behind PPI is a good one. If you borrowed some money and were then made unemployed, or were taken ill, or were unable to work due to injury, the Payment Protection Insurance was there to help make the monthly payments. Simple.

It was until the salesperson was put under pressure to sell it. You see not all insurances are claimed upon. You only claim if you are eligible. So, what happens to the premiums that are paid and not claimed upon? That's profit. In many cases, it made more profit for businesses than the interest made upon the money lent.

So, businesses incentivised sellers to lend with this insurance on top. Not for the benefits that they may provide, but for the profits of the company and then for the seller to be able to keep their job. Seriously... people lost their jobs because they were not selling enough 'products' to people who didn't want them or need them, and this is where part of the PPI mess began.

So, are you incentivising your colleagues and customers in the right ways to help build your business? Or are you risking repercussions at a later date, that may cost you more than you bargained for?

67 What are the three most critical things to the success of the business?

What are the three main drivers of your business?

What are the three main things that MUST happen for the business to be successful?

Then perhaps the follow-up question should be, what is your back up plan should any of these three not happen as you want or are predicted?

What are your backup plans if any of these should fail and how easy are they to implement?

68 Which 20% of clients account for the 80% of profit?

This is quite simply Paretto's Law which has been proven time and time and time again. 80% of your sales and profit are gotten from 20% of your clients and customers.

Which gives you a perfect profile for who your ideal customers and clients are surely?

So, note down who those customers are. Where they are. Where they hang out. What they read. What circles they move in. Study them and find out as much about them as you can. Why?

Well simply because the more you know about them, the more you'll be able to specifically market to them, the more ideal customers and clients you'll be able to get. Simple.

69 Who are your top five clients and how much contribution did they generate last month?

Two reasons I ask this.

One is fairly obvious off the back of the last question, the second not so much.

Your clients and customers are THE most important people on your payroll. Why?

Well, they can hire or fire you as quickly as anything. One moment you can be the flavour of the month, the next you are a bitter taste. Consider them employees. You need to look after them, not necessarily financially, but going the extra mile. Why?

Because they will be your best marketers for you and your business. They will run through brick walls for you. They will stand by you when times are tough and sing your praises when you do something they least expect.

So, don't you want a few more like that?

70 Which clients are unprofitable?

Everyone has an hourly rate. Everyone has costs before profit. So, I want you to really focus in on those clients that for whatever reason you spend 10 hours doing something for and only bill for 5.

Why are you doing that?

Then there are those that to solve their problem it only costs you 'x' amount, but for others costs you 'y'. Why is that?

What can you do about it?
Can you bring them into line?
Are there better ways to make these clients profitable or do you need a reality check, and ditch them? It's a business. Not a charity!

So, think...

71 Which clients would you sack?

Straight off the back of the last few questions.

Whilst they should be regarded as your best employees, they should also be looked at as some of your worst.

You know the ones?

The late payers...the ones who constantly rearrange appointments...the ones that constantly barter on price, or quality or quantity...the ones who want a Picasso in the same time it takes to do a dot-to-dot.

Yeah. Those ones.

Now you've written a list, what does your gut tell you to do?

72 Which underperforming products / services should you drop now? Why?

Every business has products and services that if you ask them, they reply without thinking that they are 'slow sellers'.

Many reasons for this, probably because they don't market them enough, or to the right people. But what if you have?

What if you've tried everything to shift it? It's time, to be honest with yourself and STOP wasting your time and money by offering it.

Every business is a problem solver...so start solving problems your customers actually have and make money rather than offering something you 'think' they have and earning nothing.

73 Which products / services should you concentrate on selling more of?

Here's an easy one.

Which products or services should you be selling more of?

Have you taken your foot off the pedal when it comes to marketing it? What's the feedback on it? Is it profitable? Is it a quick win? Does it differentiate you from your competitors?

What's stopping you from selling more?
What could you do to get over or around those hurdles?

Write down a plan on how you're going to sell more, then just put it into action...today.

74 What is success for you?

This is about you. Not your business.

What does your life look like if you are a 'success'?

Lots of money? Nice holidays? University fees paid for the kids? Debts paid off? Mortgage paid off?

Success is different for everyone. So, write down what success in your personal life looks like. Relationships, family, where you live, how you live. It's very easy to forget why you run your own business or hold a position of authority in one. This is the chance to remind yourself and make it real. Make it more tangible than the odd daydream on a coffee break.

It's also a great way to motivate yourself...because there's only one person getting in the way of your personal success. You.

Write it down and put it somewhere where you can see it every day. Use it to spur you on, remind you and focus you.

75 What is success for your business?

Your business is a tool to get that elusive personal success. So, what does success look like in your business for you to pursue your personal successes?

Are you still a one-man band?
Have you got employees? How many?
Have you got premises?
Are you on global stages, local stages, national stages?
Are you importing, exporting, buying and selling all over the world?
Are you a recognised brand or name in your industry? Locally, nationally, internationally?
What's the turnover?
What are the profits?
Where are you marketing? How are you marketing?

Write it down. Don't limit yourself to what you think you can get, write down what you really want. It's a reminder as to where you are going and just importantly, where you've come from. Many won't believe they are where they are right now, compared to when they started.

Write it down and put it somewhere we we you can see it every day. It all starts with you...

76 What does your business stand for?

Most successful businesses 'stand for' something. Let's take Apple as an example. Without getting too technical, Apple has always stood for making their customers lives easier with their devices, but stylishly.

People like to know what people and their businesses stand for. It makes them feel comfortable when they make a buying decision. It helps them with their buying decision. It's often the difference between their hands in their pocket or not.

So, what does your business stand for?
Where do you display it in your marketing content?
In some shape or form, it should be everywhere...so get to it.

77 Is the work you do, dull or exciting?

Think about it. When was the last time you laughed at work? Have you laughed today?

Or is what you do dull, monotonous and boring? (This is fine if you are an undertaker, but not much else)

Two things here. If you can't remember the last time you laughed whilst doing what you do, you may need to a) inject some fun into the business and fast or b) find something else to do.

The second thing is that customers and clients like businesses who have fun and show a sense of humour. It radiates from you to the employees to the customers. Invariably a 'happy' workplace gets more stuff done, in less time and makes it more profitable.

A happy workplace will rub off on to its customers and clients. They will enjoy buying from you, visiting you and referring you.

How can you inject more fun into your business? On the flip side, how can you calm it down if you're having too much fun and getting nothing done?

78 What will be your legacy?

If you died tomorrow and your business stopped trading with immediate effect, what legacy would it leave behind?

Every business is a problem solver. You solve problems for your customers, clients and community.

The mark of a person and a business is not what is said about when you're in the room, it's what is said when you're not. So, take that a leap further, what do you want people to say about your business and you, when you're no longer on this rock, we call Planet Earth?

Having a desire to leave a legacy, invariably propels businesses to be successful.

As Tsun Zui says in 'The Art of War'...

"It's not all about you. It starts with you."

Imagine that being said in a 'Yoda' voice and now go forth and write down what you'd like your legacy to be.

79 If your business was an animal, what would it be and why?

This is a serious question, if not slightly left field.

Is it ferocious like a tiger? Or calm and slow like a tortoise?

Is it a hybrid of different animals all rolled into one that makes it look odd, to say the least? Imagine the head of a tiger, the speed of a cheetah and the robustness of a Hippo.

Some great people to ask this question to, would be your current customers and clients. There's you, in your blissful ignorance thinking you act like the speed of a Gazelle. When in fact they see you act and deliver at the speed of a snail with housing estate of shells on its back.

It's a fun way of asking for feedback on your business. The answers have some serious lessons for you. Use them as you will...

80 What do you need to do to get your business from being the animal it is, to become the animal that you want it to be?

The natural follow on from the last question.

If your business is viewed as an old, slow, quiet tortoise, what have you got to do to make it into the young, quick, loud roaring tiger you wanted it to be?

How much work will it take?
How much money will it take?
How much do you want to make the change?

What three things can you do, today, to get the transformation underway?

Write your thoughts down and get on with it...GO!

81 Running your business is like riding a bicycle because...

Write down whatever's pops into your mind...

82 If you could work half the time you do now, what would you do to double your profit?

I almost hate to ask this question, because it seems like one of those cliched things people band around having just read their first business coaching book and think they are a coach.

But, it's a question that has its merits. If I put some context to it, you may see where it's trying to lead you. Imagine that someone in your family, suddenly became ill and dependent on you. Just you. Most people would react in a way that they would try to spin both plates. Business and doing the right thing.

So, if you could only work half the time you do now and still wanted to make the same amount of money, how would you do it? How could you make yourself more productive?

How could you double your profits, by doing half the amount of work?

It's not a dark art. It's easier than you think...

83 What would Sir Richard Branson do if he took over your business and why?

I chose Sir Richard because he's the kind of guy that would buy something today and change it tomorrow because it was good for business. But you can use a famous entrepreneur in here and ask yourself the same question.

Write down the top three things they would change and why.

Now the question is...WHY aren't you doing that NOW?

84 What would your closest rival do if they took over your business and why?

Unlike some coaches, I fully understand and have experienced that emotion is essential in either a business success or a business failure. The ones that are successful realise that they are just emotions but can see the reasons why someone feels that way about something or someone.

The ones who fail get overtaken by them. So, this is why I've asked you to think about your closest rival. It doesn't matter who you are, we all have one. Superman has Lex Luther. Batman has the Joker. It makes them tick. It pushes them on.

So, look at your business from the point of view of your closest rival. What would they change and why? Don't assume they would destroy what was good about your business, because that makes NO business sense what-so-ever. So, make the not so wild leap into thinking about what 3 things they would improve upon based on what they already do, and how they would exploit the 3 things you do well.

85 So why aren't you doing that?

It's very easy to give others advice. Very easy.

The trick is to understand WHY you've come up with these ideas, and not done anything about it in your own business. I see it countless times in the Mastermind Groups that I run.

If you write a list down of why you haven't done something and then next to it, write a list of what the benefits would be of you getting off your arse and changing things, you'll soon realise your initial thoughts are effectively, just bullshit.

Stop giving yourself excuses. Because that's all they are. Excuses. There are always ways around, under, over and through issues. Just get smarter. Learn how to do it.

You already know the benefits of changing whatever it is. The benefits will always outweigh the cost of not doing something. And if you want that extra bit of incentive, just think on this...

If you don't do it, someone else will.

86 How can you get luckier?

Ooohhh...now here's a question.

What is luck? I guess if you think about it, it's when a perfect storm happens. Everything comes together and delivers a result that you weren't expecting.

So, when it comes to business, it's pretty much about the amount of work you put in. The more times you show up; the more you offer your services; the more you promote your product; the more you solve people's problems, the 'luckier' you get.

So... how can you get luckier?

87 What excuses do you use?

You may have realised by now, that many reasons for you 'not doing stuff' are in fact, just excuses.

You may have realised you've used several of the same ones. "I'm always tired." "I haven't got time." "I don't know how." "I haven't got the money."

So, write down the excuses you use in here or on a daily basis. Now, look at them seriously. How can you overcome them?

And if your answers have 'no' in them, perhaps you don't 'want' your goals and dreams badly enough.

88 Do you have the right people around you?

You are the sum of the five closest people around you. That's what someone far wiser than me once said.

If we take that the next step, your business is the sum of you and the five closest people to it. If you have an energy zapping vampire of an accountant, you'll always hate seeing them and spend your time not listening to them seriously enough. If you have a cheap as chips printing and marketing team, you may well be putting a cheap as chips message out for your luxury product or service.

If you are surrounded by negative people that don't believe or trust in your vision and goals, guess what? You will be very unlikely to achieve them. But surround yourself with solid, go-getters and the chance increase dramatically.

So, my friend, are you surrounding yourself with the right businesses to support yours? Are you surrounding yourself with the right personal support? Who will you 'sack off'?

89 Would your business run day-to-day without you?

Here's one of those franchised cliched business coach questions. It's usually in their networking spiel somewhere.

The ideal business would run without you. Simple. That's not rocket science. A business that runs when the boss isn't there, is a business that earns the boss money whether you are on holiday or in bed fast asleep.

So what parts of your business could be automated? What parts could 'happen' if you're not around?

And if you are sat there saying, none of it, well perhaps you need to have a deeper think on whether you need to 'let go' a bit.

90 What contingency plans have you got in place should you become ill and need to take a year off?

This is a bit of a personal question and I make no apologies for asking it. As a business owner, I crashed and burned and was out of action for 9 months. It took me a year to get back to where I needed to be.

Many of us have mortgages, rent, bills and debt to pay. So, if you were involved in an accident tomorrow, how would you cope?

How would the family cope?

How would your business cope?

Give this a long hard think. Then go do something about it.

You just never know...

91 Do you avoid tough decisions?

Not one person on the planet likes confrontation. Not even Gordon Ramsay.

But if you take a look at one of the Scottish Chef's TV Programmes, you will see plenty of business owners who avoid tough and important decisions.

Avoidance, (and a certain amount of ineptitude), leads them to the verge of shutting their doors. It becomes easier to ignore problems, issues and just plain wrong business decisions because the business owner considers them a tough decision to make and would rather not make it.

We've all been there.

So, what tough decisions have you been avoiding? What things do you know that need to happen or must happen, but you are just avoiding them?

My friend, the consideration you must now have is, how are those tough decisions or lack of them going to affect your business?

92 Do you feel burned out?

Here is a stark fact. 1 in 4 people will struggle with a mental health issue this year, including stress and burn out. When you run your own business, it's more likely to be 1 in 3.

Scary isn't it? There are many reasons for it, but when you start your business, friends, family and loved ones don't actually quite 'get' the self-employed bug. They think life is easy and you can have time off when you want to.

The truth is, you probably work harder now than when someone else employed you. You probably work longer hours for no more pay. And you wake up thinking about your business and going to sleep thinking about your business. Your mental bandwidth is just taken up with business, business, business.

It's obvious you can't run at 100mph constantly before we run out of fuel. Yet we all try it.

Be kind to yourself and start thinking about downtime. Think about what you could be doing in your business and then with your diary, to give you some more downtime to spend, NOT thinking about your business.

On death beds around the world, no one has ever said: "I wish I hadn't...". They only ever say "I wish I had....". And that includes doing all the things you'd wanted to do privately as well as in business.

Be kind to yourself and recognise it. Do something about it.

I didn't. It cost me 12 months of my life. Don't lose a year; a month, a week; a day, because you ignored the signs of burnout.

93 How committed are you to the business?

Perhaps not the ideal question after the last one, but I couldn't think of anywhere else to put it. Hopefully, you are having a bit of a deep and meaningful conversation with yourself right now.

Is this where you wanted to be?

Right now. Here and now. Is this what you'd dreamed of, thought of and wanted when you started on your business journey?

You have two choices. Do nothing or commit to those goals and visions. It's amazing how many business owners I've met who say they are committed to their business and then say they can't be bothered to get up early to go networking. Or have never watched a TED video to improve their business because they'd rather watch a cat video on YouTube instead. Or don't go to Exhibitions, Workshops and Seminars because they don't see the value of looking and learning at what their peers are doing.

The ones that aren't committed to a sometimes-difficult road, probably aren't committed to their business. And as a result, will be unlikely to get anywhere near where they wanted to be.

94 When was the last time you set yourself a personal goal, that wasn't boring?

We all do it.

Spend time with kids. Go to the gym more often. See the family more often. Spend less time watching box sets on Netflix.

But when was the last time you set yourself a goal like a holiday of a lifetime? Watching your favourite team at their home ground? Seeing your favourite rock star at Wembley Stadium? Or in New York? Or in Paris?

I challenge you right now, to set yourself a personal goal that will help drive you and your business into making it happen. You could even go one stage further.

As an example, if it's the holiday or trip you are after...go and book it and put the deposit down on it. You've then got a ticking time limit to pay for the rest. Some of you do say you work better under pressure...well if you don't do it, imagine your loved one's faces...!

95 When was the last time you set yourself a business goal, that wasn't boring?

You knew this was coming.

But so many businesses set themselves sales targets, profit targets, turnover targets, blah, blah, blah.

What about something that might galvanise the business? Raising a large amount for a local charity?

What about setting yourself the goal of becoming the #1 Go-To Expert in your industry or niche for the local press and media?

What about having a major overhaul of all your social media and attract 'x amount' more viewers, fans or customers?

Do something different that will benefit the business rather than the same old, same old.

96 When was the last time you did some business training? Boosted your own capabilities?

This for me is a thorny issue. There is a figure that is kicking around the internet, (so it must be true), that 80% of business owners get to a certain level of expertise and training and just stop. In my own experience of business owners, I would say that's not far off.

That means that a minority of businesses are continuing to improve. Continuing to get better. Continuing to challenge what's out there right now. Those are the businesses that succeed. They're not looking for easier ways necessarily, they are looking for new ways to attract, educate, and retain customers and clients. On top of that, those businesses will not only be looking to solve their own problems but the problems of their customers and clients faster, better and more economically.

There is a great phrase I want to share with you as you think about this question.

"You may be on the right road. But if you stand still long enough...you'll get run over."

It's up to you.

97 When was the last time you got someone to look at your business from a different perspective?

"I help businesses work ON their business, not IN their business." I absolutely hate that phrase when coaches stand up and introduce themselves. But arguably, it is what we do.

There are so many people out there that can help you look at your business; me included. It really does help.

Why do you think World Class Golfers have caddies with them? They are there to provide another set of eyes on a particular course, hole or shot. Emotions can get in the way. Pressure can build up. And the mind reacts. Sometimes for the better, sometimes for the worse. They are there to make sure it's not for the worse.

That's why another set of eyes is important. You might be missing the obvious. You might not be seeing a problem arriving on the horizon. You may be spending a lot of time and money on doing the wrong thing at the wrong time.

So, who do you ask and how often?
Who could you approach and get started with?

98 If Lord Alan Sugar came into your business today, what would he tell you was wrong with your business?

How could you do less of it?

If you don't know who or what he is, go and have a look at 'The Apprentice'. Watch an episode. He has become a slight caricature of himself in recent seasons, so he can become 'meme-worthy', but a lot of his observation on individuals and the way they handle the weekly tasks are absolutely spot on.

He won't hold back, and neither should you. Look at what's wrong and how you can do less of it. It will immediately stop being a drag or block to your business.

99 If Lord Alan Sugar came into your business today, what would he tell you was right with your business?

How could you do more of it?

And now we have balance.

Be positive. Be proud.

Just get on and do it.

100 How could you improve it?

Of all the things that you've written down, now is the time to put it all together.

You have come up with the problems that need to be corrected. You've come up with your best assets and how to exploit and build upon them.

You are the one that's challenged your own wisdom, your own thinking and your own perspective. I just asked some questions.

So now is the time to get a plan of action together and make it happen. Otherwise, this whole exercise would have been a complete waste of time and effort.

In an odd way, it shouldn't take me to motivate you into doing things differently. Your answers to some of these questions should do.

So, what's the plan of action?
When does it start?

101 Are you, always right?

All of these questions have been building to this.

I wonder whether your answer would have been the same as now if I had asked this question at the beginning? For some, yes. For some, no.

But for those who would have answered 'yes' near the start, I hope that some of these questions have challenged your thinking and/or perspective on things personally and business-wise.

A coach should challenge. Whether it be in business or sport. It's about helping someone be the best that they can be. It's about helping a business to be the best it can be.

I use sport as an example because we look at sportsmen as pinnacles of success. Look at the £50,000,000 striker. He's worth that amount of money because someone paid that for them. But even at £50,000,000, there are ways and means of making them a £70,000,000 player. The coach helps them to use their strengths and execute those skills flawlessly more often. He acknowledges the weaknesses and helps the player improve those weak areas. The confidence grows, and the skills start to work hand in hand with each other and you end with someone who was talented and successful, becoming even more talented and even more successful. This benefits the team, who go on to win more games, more trophies and make more money in the process.

It's the same for businesses and their owners. Everyone started somewhere. The football player with a ball in the back garden. The business owner with an idea over a cup of coffee or a pint of beer.

The only thing ever standing in their way of becoming successful, has always been the individual. It's about time you became that success you always wanted to be. Let's have it!